History and Causes of Cuba's External Debt Crisis

Copyright Page

TITLE: History and Causes of Cuba's External Debt Crisis

1ST Edition

Copyright @ 2023

Roberto M. Rodriguez. All rights reserved.

ISBN: 9798223543336

Table of Contents

History and Causes of Cuba's External Debt Crisis

By Roberto Miguel Rodriguez

Chapter 1: Introduction

Background of Cuba's External Debt Crisis

Cuba's external debt crisis has been a topic of great concern among bankers and financial experts in recent years. This subchapter aims to provide a comprehensive understanding of the background behind Cuba's external debt crisis, shedding light on the history and causes that have led to this predicament.

Cuba's external debt, delinquencies, and refinancing difficulties have had a significant impact on the country's economic development. The accumulation of debt over the years has hindered Cuba's ability to attract foreign investment and finance its domestic development projects. This subchapter will explore the various factors that have contributed to the country's debt crisis, including economic mismanagement, political instability, and international economic sanctions.

The Cuban government's strategies for managing external debt and delinquencies have been a crucial aspect of its response to the crisis. This subchapter will delve into the policies and measures implemented by the government to address the debt crisis, including debt restructuring, negotiation processes with creditors, and seeking assistance from international financial institutions. It will provide an analysis of the effectiveness of these strategies and their implications for the country's long-term sustainability.

The implications of Cuba's external debt on social welfare and public services cannot be understated. The high debt burden has limited the government's ability to allocate sufficient resources to essential sectors such as education, healthcare, and infrastructure development. This subchapter will examine the impact of the debt crisis on the provision of public services and the overall well-being of the Cuban people.

Furthermore, this subchapter will explore the role of international financial institutions in Cuba's debt refinancing efforts. It will analyze the assistance provided by these institutions and evaluate their effectiveness in helping Cuba overcome its debt crisis.

The external debt crisis has also had a significant effect on foreign direct investment in Cuba. This subchapter will examine how the high debt burden has deterred foreign investors, leading to a decline in much-needed capital inflows. It will also discuss potential solutions to attract foreign investment and promote economic growth in the country.

Additionally, the impact of Cuba's external debt on domestic inflation and currency stability will be explored. The subchapter will analyze how the debt crisis has affected the country's inflation rate and exchange rate, and the potential risks it poses to macroeconomic stability.

The implications of Cuba's external debt on the country's credit rating will also be examined. This subchapter will discuss how the debt crisis has affected Cuba's creditworthiness and its ability to access international financial markets.

Finally, this subchapter will provide an analysis of Cuba's debt restructuring and negotiation processes with creditors. It will assess the challenges faced by the country in reaching agreements with its creditors and the potential implications of these agreements on Cuba's long-term financial stability.

In conclusion, this subchapter will provide a comprehensive analysis of the background behind Cuba's external debt crisis. It will explore the history and causes of the crisis, the strategies employed by the Cuban government to manage the debt, and the implications of the crisis on various aspects of the country's economy. It will also discuss potential solutions for long-term sustainability and offer insights into the future prospects for Cuba's external debt.

Importance of Understanding the Causes and History of Cuba's External Debt Crisis

The Importance of Understanding the Causes and History of Cuba's External Debt Crisis

Introduction:

The external debt crisis experienced by Cuba has had far-reaching implications on its economy, social welfare, and credit rating. As bankers, it is crucial to comprehend the causes and history behind this crisis to make informed decisions and devise effective strategies. This subchapter aims to shed light on the significance of understanding Cuba's external debt crisis and its various aspects.

Cuba's External Debt, Delinquencies, and Refinancing Difficulties:

Understanding the intricacies of Cuba's external debt is vital for bankers dealing with the country. Delinquencies and refinancing difficulties have been persistent challenges for the Cuban government. By analyzing these issues, bankers can better assess the risks associated with lending to or investing in Cuba.

The Impact on Economic Development:

Cuba's external debt crisis has hindered its economic development. Bankers need to comprehend the extent of this impact to make informed decisions regarding investment opportunities and lending practices. By understanding the link between external debt and economic development, bankers can effectively assess the potential returns on investment.

The History and Causes of Cuba's External Debt Crisis:

Studying the history and causes of Cuba's external debt crisis provides valuable insights for bankers. It allows them to identify patterns, evaluate risk factors, and anticipate future challenges. By understanding the root causes, bankers can design strategies to mitigate risks and enhance their financial operations in Cuba.

Cuban Government's Strategies for Managing External Debt and Delinquencies:

Bankers need to be aware of the strategies employed by the Cuban government to manage external debt and delinquencies. This knowledge enables them to align their lending policies and negotiate favorable terms. By understanding the government's approach, bankers can build stronger partnerships and contribute to sustainable solutions.

Implications on Social Welfare and Public Services:

Cuba's external debt crisis directly impacts social welfare and public services. Bankers must comprehend these implications to gauge the overall economic stability and potential risks. By considering the social impact, bankers can ensure responsible lending practices and contribute to the welfare of Cuban citizens.

Role of International Financial Institutions in Debt Refinancing Efforts:

International financial institutions play a crucial role in Cuba's debt refinancing efforts. Bankers need to understand their involvement, policies, and procedures to navigate the financial landscape effectively. By collaborating with these institutions, bankers can contribute to the successful refinancing of Cuba's external debt.

Conclusion:

Understanding the causes and history of Cuba's external debt crisis is of utmost importance for bankers. It allows them to assess risks, devise effective strategies, and contribute to sustainable economic development. By analyzing various aspects, such as the impact on economic development, social welfare, and credit rating, bankers can make informed decisions and foster long-term partnerships with Cuba.

Objectives of the Book

The subchapter "Objectives of the Book" in "Unraveling the History and Causes of Cuba's External Debt Crisis: A Banker's Perspective" aims to provide bankers with a comprehensive understanding of Cuba's external debt crisis. The book addresses various niches within the topic, ensuring a thorough exploration of the subject matter.

Firstly, the book intends to delve into the history and causes of Cuba's external debt crisis. It examines the factors that led to the accumulation of debt and the subsequent challenges faced by the Cuban economy. By providing a detailed analysis, bankers can gain valuable insights into the root causes of the crisis.

Moreover, the book aims to shed light on Cuba's external debt and its impact on economic development. It explores how the debt burden has hindered the country's economic growth and development prospects. Bankers can gain a nuanced understanding of the relationship between debt and economic progress, enabling them to make informed decisions and develop appropriate strategies.

Additionally, the book examines the Cuban government's strategies for managing external debt and delinquencies. It analyzes the measures taken by the government to address the challenges posed by debt and delinquencies. This insight equips bankers with knowledge of the Cuban government's approach, enabling them to evaluate the effectiveness of these strategies and their implications for the financial sector.

Furthermore, the book explores the implications of Cuba's external debt on social welfare and public services. It examines how the debt crisis has affected the provision of essential services to the Cuban population. By understanding the social consequences, bankers can assess the broader impact of the crisis and its implications for the country's stability.

The role of international financial institutions in Cuba's debt refinancing efforts is also analyzed in the book. It delves into the involvement of organizations such as the International Monetary Fund and the World Bank in assisting Cuba with debt refinancing. Bankers can gain insights into the role of these institutions and their contributions to the resolution of Cuba's debt crisis.

Furthermore, the book examines how Cuba's external debt has affected foreign direct investment and the overall investment climate. It explores the impact of the debt crisis on investor confidence and the challenges faced by foreign companies operating in Cuba. Bankers can gain a comprehensive understanding of the relationship between debt and foreign investment, enabling them to make informed decisions regarding investment opportunities in Cuba.

Moreover, the book explores the impact of Cuba's external debt on domestic inflation and currency stability. It examines how the debt burden has influenced inflation rates and currency value, affecting the stability of the Cuban economy. Bankers can gain insights into these macroeconomic factors, allowing them to assess the risks and opportunities associated with lending and investment in Cuba.

In addition, the book analyzes the implications of Cuba's external debt for the country's credit rating. It examines how the debt crisis has affected Cuba's creditworthiness and its ability to access international financial markets. Bankers can gain a comprehensive understanding of the credit implications and evaluate the risks associated with lending to or investing in Cuba.

Furthermore, the book provides an in-depth analysis of Cuba's debt restructuring and negotiation processes with creditors. It explores the strategies adopted by the Cuban government to renegotiate debt terms and alleviate the burden. Bankers can gain insights into these processes, enabling them to participate in future debt restructuring efforts and make informed decisions regarding debt negotiations.

Lastly, the book discusses the future prospects for Cuba's external debt and potential solutions for long-term sustainability. It explores possible strategies and policies that can help Cuba overcome its debt crisis and achieve sustainable economic growth. Bankers can gain valuable insights into the future trajectory of Cuba's external debt, allowing them to develop strategies that align with the country's long-term goals.

In conclusion, the objectives of the book "Unraveling the History and Causes of Cuba's External Debt Crisis: A Banker's Perspective" are to provide bankers with a comprehensive understanding of Cuba's external debt crisis. It addresses various niches within the topic, ensuring a thorough exploration of the subject matter and equipping bankers with the knowledge and insights necessary to make informed decisions and develop appropriate strategies.

Chapter 2: Cuba's External Debt

Overview of Cuba's External Debt

Cuba's external debt has been a topic of great concern and interest, particularly among bankers who closely monitor the country's financial situation. In this subchapter, we will provide an overview of Cuba's external debt, exploring its history, causes, and implications for the country's economic development.

Cuba's external debt is a result of years of borrowing from foreign creditors to finance its economic activities and development projects. Over the years, the country has accumulated a substantial amount of debt, and this has become a major challenge for the Cuban government. Delinquencies and refinancing difficulties have plagued the country, making it increasingly difficult for Cuba to meet its financial obligations.

The external debt crisis in Cuba has had a significant impact on the country's economic development. The high debt burdens have limited the government's ability to invest in infrastructure development, social welfare programs, and public services. This has led to a decline in the quality of life for many Cubans and has hindered the country's overall economic growth.

To manage external debt and delinquencies, the Cuban government has implemented various strategies. These include debt restructuring, negotiation processes with creditors, and seeking financial assistance from international financial institutions. The role of these institutions, such as the International Monetary Fund and the World Bank, in Cuba's debt refinancing efforts is crucial for the country's financial stability.

Cuba's external debt also has implications for foreign direct investment. The high levels of debt make investors cautious, as they worry about the country's ability to repay its debts. This, in turn, affects the inflow of foreign capital, which is vital for Cuba's economic growth and development.

Furthermore, the country's external debt has an impact on domestic inflation and currency stability. The government faces the challenge of balancing debt repayments with the need to maintain price stability and prevent currency devaluation. This delicate balance requires careful management and economic planning.

The external debt crisis in Cuba has also affected the country's credit rating, making it difficult for the government to access international financial markets at favorable interest rates. This further exacerbates the challenges faced by the Cuban economy.

In analyzing Cuba's debt restructuring and negotiation processes with creditors, it is crucial to consider the long-term sustainability of the country's external debt. Potential solutions for sustainable debt management include debt forgiveness, debt-for-equity swaps, and promoting economic reforms that stimulate growth and increase export revenues.

Looking ahead, the future prospects for Cuba's external debt will depend on the effectiveness of the government's strategies for managing debt and delinquencies. Sustainable economic growth, increased foreign investment, and improved credit ratings will be key factors in resolving Cuba's external debt crisis and ensuring long-term financial stability for the country.

Factors Influencing Cuba's External Debt Levels

Cuba's external debt crisis is a complex issue that has unfolded over several decades, and understanding the factors that have influenced the country's debt levels is crucial for bankers and professionals in the finance industry. This subchapter aims to delve into the key factors that have contributed to Cuba's external debt, providing valuable insights into the country's economic situation and potential solutions for long-term sustainability.

One of the primary factors influencing Cuba's external debt levels is the country's historical reliance on foreign borrowing. Since the Cuban Revolution in 1959, the government has pursued an economic model that heavily relies on imports, leading to a continuous need for foreign loans to finance these purchases. This dependency on external financing has contributed to the accumulation of significant debt over time.

Another factor is the impact of economic mismanagement and policy inefficiencies. Cuba's centrally planned economy has led to inefficiencies in resource allocation and a lack of incentives for productivity, resulting in weak economic performance. This, coupled with the country's limited access to international markets due to political reasons, has further strained its ability to service its external debt.

The Cuban government's strategies for managing external debt and delinquencies have also played a role in the country's debt crisis. Despite facing financial difficulties, the government has prioritized social welfare and public services, diverting funds away from debt repayment. While this may have positive implications for the population, it has hindered the country's ability to meet its financial obligations.

International financial institutions, such as the International Monetary Fund (IMF) and the World Bank, have also impacted Cuba's debt refinancing efforts. Due to political disagreements and ideological differences, Cuba has faced limited access to financial assistance from these institutions, forcing the country to seek alternative sources of financing and negotiate with creditors on its own terms.

Furthermore, Cuba's external debt has had a significant impact on its economic development, foreign direct investment, inflation rates, currency stability, and credit rating. The country's high debt levels have deterred foreign investors, as they perceive increased risks and uncertainties. Additionally, the need to service external debt has put pressure on the government's ability to prioritize domestic investment and infrastructure development.

In conclusion, understanding the factors that have influenced Cuba's external debt levels is crucial for bankers and professionals in the finance industry. Factors such as historical reliance on foreign borrowing, economic mismanagement, government strategies, the role of international financial institutions, and the impact on economic development and stability have all contributed to Cuba's external debt crisis. By analyzing these factors, bankers can gain valuable insights into the country's economic situation and explore potential solutions for long-term sustainability.

Types of Debt Instruments and Creditors Involved

In understanding the complexities of Cuba's external debt crisis, it is crucial to delve into the different types of debt instruments and the creditors involved. This subchapter aims to provide a comprehensive overview of these aspects from a banker's perspective.

Cuba's external debt comprises various debt instruments, each with its own characteristics and implications. One prominent type is sovereign debt, which is issued by the Cuban government to finance its development projects and meet its financial obligations. This includes bonds, which are long-term debt securities with fixed interest rates and maturity dates. Bonds are typically sold to institutional investors such as pension funds and insurance companies.

Another type of debt instrument is commercial loans, which are obtained from commercial banks and financial institutions. These loans are often used to fund specific projects or to meet short-term financing needs. Additionally, Cuba has relied on multilateral loans from international financial institutions such as the World Bank and the International Monetary Fund (IMF). These loans come with conditions and strict repayment schedules.

Regarding the creditors involved, Cuba's external debt has been owed to a diverse range of entities. Traditional creditors include other governments and international organizations, while private creditors such as commercial banks and bondholders also play a significant role. In recent years, Cuba has sought debt relief from its creditors, leading to negotiations with creditor committees and ad hoc groups.

The involvement of international financial institutions in Cuba's debt refinancing efforts cannot be overlooked. These institutions have often provided technical assistance and financial support to help Cuba manage its debt burden. They have also played a crucial role in facilitating debt restructuring and negotiation processes between Cuba and its creditors.

Understanding the types of debt instruments and creditors involved is essential in analyzing the causes and implications of Cuba's external debt crisis. It sheds light on the challenges faced by the Cuban government in managing its debt and delinquencies. Moreover, it provides insights into the impact of Cuba's external debt on economic development, social welfare, foreign direct investment, inflation, currency stability, and credit ratings.

By comprehending the intricacies of Cuba's debt instruments and the creditors involved, bankers can better evaluate the risks and opportunities associated with Cuba's external debt. This knowledge can assist in formulating strategies for debt restructuring, negotiation, and long-term sustainability. Ultimately, it allows bankers to contribute to the future prospects of Cuba's external debt and explore potential solutions for its economic development.

Chapter 3: Delinquencies and Refinancing Difficulties

Analysis of Cuba's Debt Delinquencies

Cuba's external debt crisis has been a topic of great concern for bankers and financial institutions worldwide. This subchapter will delve into the analysis of Cuba's debt delinquencies, providing valuable insights into the history, causes, and implications of this ongoing crisis.

One of the key aspects to understand about Cuba's external debt is the impact it has had on the country's economic development. The accumulation of debt has hindered Cuba's ability to invest in crucial sectors such as infrastructure, education, and healthcare. As a result, the country's social welfare and public services have been compromised, leading to a decline in the overall quality of life for its citizens.

The Cuban government has employed various strategies to manage its external debt and delinquencies. These strategies include debt restructuring and negotiation processes with creditors. However, the effectiveness of these measures has been limited, and Cuba continues to face challenges in meeting its debt obligations.

The role of international financial institutions in Cuba's debt refinancing efforts is another crucial aspect to consider. These institutions have played a significant role in providing financial assistance and guidance to help Cuba navigate its debt crisis. However, the effectiveness of their efforts has been questioned, and alternative solutions for long-term sustainability need to be explored.

Cuba's external debt has also had a profound effect on foreign direct investment in the country. Investors are wary of committing resources to a nation burdened with high debt and limited economic stability. This has hindered Cuba's ability to attract much-needed foreign investment, which could have played a crucial role in stimulating economic growth.

Furthermore, the impact of Cuba's external debt on domestic inflation and currency stability cannot be overlooked. The country has experienced inflationary pressures due to its inability to manage its debt effectively, resulting in a devaluation of its currency. This has created additional challenges for the Cuban economy, further exacerbating the debt crisis.

The implications of Cuba's external debt on the country's credit rating are also significant. The accumulation of debt has led to a downgrade in Cuba's creditworthiness, making it increasingly difficult for the country to access credit in international markets. This, in turn, limits its ability to refinance its debt and exacerbates the crisis.

In conclusion, the analysis of Cuba's debt delinquencies highlights the complex challenges the country faces in managing its external debt. The impact on economic development, social welfare, and public services, as well as the implications for foreign direct investment, credit rating, and domestic inflation, are significant. It is crucial for bankers and financial institutions to understand these dynamics to explore potential solutions for long-term debt sustainability and support Cuba's economic recovery.

Challenges Faced by Cuba in Refinancing its Debt

Cuba, a nation grappling with a long history of external debt, has been facing numerous challenges in refinancing its debt. These challenges have significant implications for the country's economic development and the welfare of its citizens. In this subchapter, we will explore the key obstacles that Cuba faces in its efforts to refinance its debt and the potential solutions for long-term sustainability.

One of the primary challenges facing Cuba is the delinquencies and refinancing difficulties it encounters. The country has struggled to meet its debt obligations, resulting in a deteriorating credit profile and limited access to international capital markets. This has made it incredibly challenging for Cuba to secure favorable terms for refinancing its debt and has further exacerbated its financial woes.

Moreover, Cuba's external debt burden has had a profound impact on its economic development. The country's debt obligations have diverted a significant portion of its resources away from essential public services and social welfare programs. As a result, the Cuban government has been forced to prioritize debt repayment over domestic investment, leading to a stagnation in economic growth and a decline in living standards for its citizens.

In its efforts to manage external debt and delinquencies, the Cuban government has implemented various strategies. These include engaging in debt restructuring and negotiation processes with creditors, seeking financial assistance from international financial institutions, and exploring alternative sources of financing. However, these strategies have proven to be challenging due to the country's limited access to capital markets and its strained relations with international financial institutions.

The implications of Cuba's external debt on foreign direct investment (FDI) and domestic inflation are also significant. The high levels of debt and the uncertainty surrounding its repayment have deterred foreign investors from entering the Cuban market. Furthermore, the country's debt burden has put pressure on its domestic currency, leading to inflation and currency instability.

Cuba's external debt crisis has also had implications for the country's credit rating. The deteriorating credit profile has resulted in downgrades by credit rating agencies, making it even more challenging for the country to attract foreign investment and secure favorable refinancing terms.

Looking ahead, the future prospects for Cuba's external debt depend on its ability to implement sustainable solutions. Long-term sustainability can be achieved through a combination of debt restructuring, improved governance, and economic reforms aimed at attracting foreign investment and diversifying the economy. Additionally, strengthening relations with international financial institutions and improving transparency in debt management will be crucial for Cuba's debt refinancing efforts.

In conclusion, Cuba faces numerous challenges in refinancing its debt. The delinquencies and refinancing difficulties, coupled with the impact on economic development, social welfare, and public services, pose significant obstacles for the country. However, through strategic debt restructuring, negotiation processes, and sustainable economic reforms, Cuba can work towards long-term sustainability and mitigate the adverse effects of its external debt crisis.

Impact of Delinquencies and Refinancing Difficulties on the Economy

Title: Impact of Delinquencies and Refinancing Difficulties on the Economy

Introduction:

In this subchapter, we will explore the profound impact of delinquencies and refinancing difficulties on Cuba's economy within the context of its external debt crisis. As bankers, understanding these intricacies is crucial for comprehending the challenges and opportunities that lie ahead. We will delve into the history, causes, and implications of Cuba's external debt crisis, as well as the strategies employed by the Cuban government. Additionally, we will examine the role of international financial institutions, the effect on social welfare and public services, foreign direct investment, domestic inflation, currency stability, credit rating, debt restructuring, and negotiation processes. Lastly, we will discuss potential solutions for long-term sustainability.

1. The History and Causes of Cuba's External Debt Crisis:

To comprehend the present situation, we must understand the historical context and underlying factors that contributed to Cuba's external debt crisis. We will examine the economic policies, political circumstances, and global events that led to this predicament.

2. Cuban Government's Strategies for Managing External Debt and Delinquencies:

The Cuban government has implemented several strategies to manage its external debt and delinquencies. We will analyze their approaches, including debt rescheduling, debt-for-equity swaps, and debt buybacks, and evaluate their effectiveness in addressing the crisis.

3. Implications of Cuba's External Debt on Social Welfare and Public Services:

The burden of external debt has significant implications for social welfare and public services in Cuba. We will explore how limited resources and debt servicing obligations affect the provision of healthcare, education, and other essential public services.

4. The Role of International Financial Institutions in Cuba's Debt Refinancing Efforts:

International financial institutions play a crucial role in Cuba's debt refinancing efforts. We will discuss the involvement of institutions such as the International Monetary Fund, World Bank, and regional development banks, and their impact on Cuba's economic stability.

5. The Impact of Cuba's External Debt on Foreign Direct Investment (FDI):

Cuba's external debt crisis has implications for foreign direct investment. We will analyze how high debt levels and payment difficulties affect investor confidence and the inflow of FDI, which is critical for economic growth and development.

6. Cuba's External Debt and Its Effect on Domestic Inflation and Currency Stability:

The level of external debt can exert pressure on domestic inflation and currency stability. We will examine how debt servicing obligations impact the value of the Cuban peso, inflation rates, and overall economic stability.

7. Cuba's External Debt and Its Implications for the Country's Credit Rating:

The level of external debt is closely linked to a country's credit rating. We will assess how Cuba's debt crisis influences its creditworthiness, borrowing costs, and access to international financial markets.

8. Analysis of Cuba's Debt Restructuring and Negotiation Processes with Creditors:

Cuba has engaged in debt restructuring and negotiations with its creditors. We will analyze the outcomes of these processes, the terms agreed upon, and their impact on Cuba's debt sustainability.

9. The Future Prospects for Cuba's External Debt and Potential Solutions for Long-term Sustainability:

Finally, we will explore the future prospects for Cuba's external debt and potential solutions for achieving long-term debt sustainability. We will discuss debt reduction strategies, economic reforms, and the role of international cooperation in supporting Cuba's journey towards economic stability.

Conclusion:

Understanding the impact of delinquencies and refinancing difficulties on Cuba's economy is crucial for bankers navigating the complex landscape of Cuba's external debt crisis. By comprehending the historical context, causes, and implications, we can better assess the challenges and opportunities that lie ahead and explore sustainable solutions for long-term economic growth in Cuba.

Chapter 4: Impact on Economic Development

Relationship between Cuba's External Debt and Economic Development

Cuba's external debt has played a significant role in shaping the country's economic development over the years. This subchapter aims to explore the intricate relationship between Cuba's external debt and its impact on economic development. As bankers, it is crucial to understand the dynamics of Cuba's external debt crisis and the implications it has on various facets of the country's economy.

The history and causes of Cuba's external debt crisis lay the foundation for comprehending its current state. By delving into the historical context, we can identify the main factors that led to the accumulation of debt and the subsequent challenges faced by the Cuban government. Understanding these causes will provide valuable insights into the complexities of managing external debt and delinquencies.

One of the key aspects to be examined is the Cuban government's strategies for managing external debt and delinquencies. By analyzing their approach, bankers can gain a deeper understanding of the measures taken to alleviate the debt burden and mitigate the risks associated with delinquencies. This knowledge will inform decision-making processes and facilitate effective engagement with the Cuban government.

The implications of Cuba's external debt on social welfare and public services are also of utmost importance. Bankers must recognize the impact that a high external debt burden can have on the availability and quality of public services. A comprehensive analysis of this relationship will allow for a better assessment of the country's social and economic well-being.

Another critical aspect to explore is the role of international financial institutions in Cuba's debt refinancing efforts. By understanding the involvement of these institutions, bankers can gain insights into the potential opportunities and challenges that arise during the debt restructuring and negotiation processes.

Additionally, this subchapter will delve into the effect of Cuba's external debt on foreign direct investment, domestic inflation, and currency stability. These factors are closely interlinked and can significantly influence the country's economic development. Evaluating these relationships will aid bankers in assessing the risks and opportunities associated with investing in Cuba.

Furthermore, the subchapter will analyze the implications of Cuba's external debt on the country's credit rating. A thorough examination of this relationship will provide important insights into the country's creditworthiness and its ability to access international financial markets.

Finally, this subchapter will conclude with an exploration of the future prospects for Cuba's external debt and potential solutions for long-term sustainability. By considering the current economic climate and the challenges faced by the Cuban government, bankers can identify potential strategies and avenues for sustainable debt management.

In conclusion, this subchapter aims to provide bankers with a comprehensive understanding of the relationship between Cuba's external debt and economic development. By exploring various aspects such as the historical context, strategies for debt management, and implications on social welfare, bankers can make informed decisions and contribute to the sustainable development of Cuba's economy.

Effects of Debt Burden on Key Economic Indicators

The effects of debt burden on key economic indicators are of utmost importance to bankers, especially when it comes to countries facing external debt crises, such as Cuba. Understanding these effects is crucial for developing strategies to manage delinquencies, facilitate refinancing, and ultimately promote economic development.

One of the primary consequences of a high debt burden is the strain it puts on a country's economic development. Cuba's external debt has had a significant impact on its ability to invest in key sectors, such as infrastructure, education, and healthcare. Limited resources are allocated towards debt repayment, leaving little room for public investment, which hampers social welfare and public services.

Furthermore, the weight of external debt affects a nation's credit rating. Cuba's credibility in the global financial market is undermined due to its rising debt levels, leading to higher borrowing costs. This, in turn, limits the country's access to international financial markets and foreign direct investment, which are crucial for sustainable economic growth.

Additionally, high levels of external debt can lead to domestic inflation and currency instability. As a country borrows more to finance its obligations, the money supply increases, leading to higher prices and reduced purchasing power. This can create a vicious cycle as inflation erodes the value of the local currency, further exacerbating the debt burden.

To tackle these challenges, the Cuban government has employed various strategies to manage external debt and delinquencies. This includes debt restructuring and negotiation processes with creditors, seeking the support of international financial institutions, and exploring potential solutions for long-term sustainability.

The role of international financial institutions, such as the International Monetary Fund and the World Bank, is crucial in assisting Cuba's debt refinancing efforts. These institutions can provide technical expertise, financial support, and guidance on effective debt management practices.

Looking into the future, it is essential to analyze Cuba's debt restructuring efforts and assess their impact on key economic indicators. By evaluating the country's current situation and potential solutions, bankers can gain insights into the future prospects for Cuba's external debt and its implications for long-term sustainability.

In conclusion, the effects of debt burden on key economic indicators are far-reaching and have significant implications for a country like Cuba. Bankers must understand the relationship between external debt, economic development, social welfare, credit rating, inflation, and currency stability to devise effective strategies and promote long-term sustainability.

Case Studies: How Cuba's External Debt Crisis Impacted Economic Development

Introduction:

In this subchapter, we will delve into the case studies that highlight the profound impact of Cuba's external debt crisis on its economic development. By examining the history, causes, and implications of this crisis, we aim to provide bankers with a comprehensive understanding of the challenges faced by Cuba and the potential solutions for long-term sustainability.

Historical Context:

To comprehend the gravity of Cuba's external debt crisis, it is crucial to examine its historical backdrop. We will explore the events that led to the accumulation of significant debt, including the country's economic policies, international relationships, and geopolitical factors. By analyzing these factors, bankers can gain valuable insights into the root causes of the crisis.

Implications for Economic Development:

Cuba's external debt crisis has had far-reaching consequences on its economic development. We will investigate how the burden of debt has hindered the country's ability to invest in crucial sectors such as healthcare, education, and infrastructure. By understanding these implications, bankers can evaluate the long-term consequences of high external debt on social welfare and public services.

Management Strategies and Negotiations:

The Cuban government has implemented various strategies to manage external debt and delinquencies. We will examine these strategies, including debt restructuring and negotiation processes with creditors. By analyzing the effectiveness of these measures, bankers can gain insights into the challenges faced by the government and the potential solutions to alleviate the crisis.

Role of International Financial Institutions:

International financial institutions play a vital role in Cuba's debt refinancing efforts. We will explore the involvement of organizations such as the International Monetary Fund and the World Bank in providing financial assistance and guidance to Cuba. By understanding their role, bankers can evaluate the impact of these institutions on the country's debt management and economic development.

Effects on Foreign Direct Investment and Currency Stability:

Cuba's external debt crisis has also affected foreign direct investment and currency stability. We will analyze how the high debt burden has deterred foreign investors and impacted the stability of the Cuban currency. By understanding these effects, bankers can assess the potential risks and opportunities associated with investing in Cuba.

Implications for Credit Rating and Inflation:

The impact of external debt on Cuba's credit rating and domestic inflation is another crucial aspect to explore. We will analyze how the debt crisis has influenced the country's creditworthiness and affected inflation rates. By understanding these implications, bankers can make informed decisions regarding risk assessment and market opportunities.

Future Prospects and Sustainable Solutions:

Finally, we will discuss the future prospects for Cuba's external debt and potential solutions for long-term sustainability. By examining the country's economic policies, diversification efforts, and international collaborations, bankers can assess the viability of long-term solutions to alleviate the debt crisis and promote economic development.

Conclusion:

By studying the case studies of Cuba's external debt crisis and its impact on economic development, bankers can gain valuable insights into the challenges faced by the country. This subchapter aims to equip bankers with the knowledge necessary to navigate the complexities of Cuba's debt crisis and contribute to sustainable solutions that promote economic growth and stability.

Chapter 5: History and Causes of Cuba's External Debt Crisis

Historical Overview of Cuba's External Debt

Cuba's external debt has been a pressing issue for many years, as the country has faced numerous challenges in managing its debt obligations. In this subchapter, we will delve into the historical overview of Cuba's external debt, providing a comprehensive understanding of the factors that have contributed to the country's current debt crisis.

Cuba's external debt can be traced back to the early 1960s when the country experienced a significant shift in its political and economic landscape. Following the Cuban Revolution, the government implemented a series of policies that led to the nationalization of industries and the restructuring of the economy. These actions, while aimed at creating a more equitable society, had a detrimental effect on Cuba's external debt.

During the 1970s and 1980s, Cuba relied heavily on loans from foreign governments and international financial institutions to finance its development projects. This led to a rapid increase in external debt, as the country sought to modernize its infrastructure and improve its social welfare programs. However, the economic downturn in the 1990s, exacerbated by the collapse of the Soviet Union, had a severe impact on Cuba's ability to service its debt.

The delinquencies and refinancing difficulties faced by Cuba further exacerbated its external debt crisis. The country struggled to meet its debt obligations, leading to a decline in its creditworthiness and limited access to international capital markets. The Cuban government implemented various strategies to manage its external debt, including debt restructuring and negotiation processes with creditors.

The implications of Cuba's external debt on economic development have been far-reaching. The country has faced constraints in funding essential public services and social welfare programs, leading to a decline in living standards for its citizens. Additionally, Cuba's external debt has had a significant impact on foreign direct investment, as potential investors have been wary of the country's unstable financial situation.

International financial institutions have played a crucial role in Cuba's debt refinancing efforts. Organizations such as the International Monetary Fund and the World Bank have provided financial aid and technical assistance to help the country navigate its debt crisis. However, the effectiveness of these efforts has been limited, and Cuba continues to face significant challenges in achieving long-term debt sustainability.

The impact of Cuba's external debt on domestic inflation and currency stability cannot be overlooked. The country has experienced high inflation rates, making it difficult for businesses and consumers to plan for the future. Additionally, currency instability has deterred foreign investors and hindered economic growth.

Cuba's external debt also has implications for the country's credit rating. The high levels of debt and ongoing delinquencies have resulted in downgrades by credit rating agencies, further restricting the country's access to international financing.

Looking ahead, Cuba's future prospects for external debt remain uncertain. However, potential solutions for long-term sustainability include implementing structural reforms to improve the business environment, attracting foreign direct investment, diversifying the economy, and strengthening debt management practices.

In conclusion, understanding the historical overview of Cuba's external debt is crucial in comprehending the country's current debt crisis. The impact on economic development, social welfare, and public services, as well as the role of international financial institutions, debt restructuring processes, and potential solutions for long-term sustainability, are all essential factors in addressing Cuba's external debt challenges.

Key Events and Factors Leading to the Debt Crisis

The debt crisis that Cuba currently faces has been the result of a series of key events and factors that have had a significant impact on the country's economy. Understanding these events and factors is crucial for bankers and those interested in Cuba's external debt to gain insight into the causes of the crisis and potential solutions for long-term sustainability.

One of the key events that contributed to Cuba's debt crisis was the collapse of the Soviet Union in 1991. As Cuba heavily relied on economic and financial support from the Soviet Union, its sudden dissolution left the country in a dire economic situation. The loss of its main trading partner and source of financial aid led to a severe economic contraction and a significant increase in external debt.

Another factor that played a role in the debt crisis was the high level of delinquencies and refinancing difficulties. Cuba struggled to meet its debt obligations, resulting in a growing number of delinquencies and difficulties in refinancing its debt. This further exacerbated the country's financial situation, making it harder to attract foreign investment and access international financial markets.

The Cuban government's strategies for managing external debt and delinquencies also contributed to the crisis. Rather than implementing comprehensive debt restructuring measures, the government resorted to short-term solutions such as debt rescheduling and debt-for-equity swaps. These strategies provided temporary relief but did not address the root causes of the debt crisis, leading to a cycle of recurring debt problems.

The impact of Cuba's external debt on economic development and social welfare cannot be overstated. The country's limited resources were increasingly diverted towards servicing its external debt, leaving little room for investment in infrastructure, education, healthcare, and other public services. This had a detrimental effect on the overall well-being of the Cuban population and hindered economic development.

The role of international financial institutions in Cuba's debt refinancing efforts also deserves attention. Despite the country's limited access to international financial markets, it sought assistance from institutions such as the International Monetary Fund (IMF) and the World Bank. However, the conditions attached to this assistance often required Cuba to implement austerity measures and economic reforms, which further strained the economy and exacerbated social inequalities.

In conclusion, a combination of key events and factors, such as the collapse of the Soviet Union, delinquencies and refinancing difficulties, the Cuban government's strategies, and the impact on economic development and social welfare, have contributed to Cuba's external debt crisis. Understanding these factors is crucial for bankers and those interested in finding potential solutions for long-term sustainability. By analyzing the history and causes of the crisis and evaluating Cuba's debt restructuring and negotiation processes, it becomes possible to assess the future prospects for the country's external debt and explore viable solutions moving forward.

Analysis of the Root Causes of the Crisis

In this subchapter, we will delve into a comprehensive analysis of the root causes that have led to Cuba's external debt crisis. As bankers, it is crucial for us to understand the underlying factors that have contributed to this crisis in order to effectively address the challenges faced by Cuba and develop sustainable solutions.

Cuba's External Debt, Delinquencies, and Refinancing Difficulties

One of the key aspects we will explore is the magnitude and composition of Cuba's external debt. We will examine the factors that have contributed to the accumulation of this debt, including borrowing patterns, economic policies, and external shocks. Additionally, we will analyze the reasons behind the delinquencies and refinancing difficulties that Cuba has encountered, seeking to understand the systemic issues at play.

Cuba's External Debt and Its Impact on Economic Development

The relationship between Cuba's external debt and its economic development is a crucial topic to explore. By examining the historical trends and patterns, we will evaluate the impact of the debt burden on economic growth, infrastructure development, and investment prospects. This analysis will provide valuable insights into the challenges that Cuba faces in achieving sustainable economic development.

The History and Causes of Cuba's External Debt Crisis

To understand the current debt crisis, it is essential to examine its historical context. We will trace the origins of Cuba's external debt crisis, exploring the factors that have contributed to its escalation over time. By identifying the key turning points and policy decisions, we can gain a deeper understanding of the causes behind this crisis.

Cuban Government's Strategies for Managing External Debt and Delinquencies

In this section, we will analyze the strategies employed by the Cuban government in managing its external debt and delinquencies. By evaluating the effectiveness of these strategies, we can identify areas for improvement and potential solutions for long-term debt sustainability.

Implications of Cuba's External Debt on Social Welfare and Public Services

The impact of Cuba's external debt on social welfare and public services is an important aspect to consider. We will assess how the debt burden has affected the provision of healthcare, education, and other essential services. By understanding these implications, we can better assess the social and human costs of the crisis.

The Role of International Financial Institutions in Cuba's Debt Refinancing Efforts

International financial institutions play a crucial role in assisting countries in debt restructuring and refinancing. We will evaluate the involvement of these institutions in Cuba's debt refinancing efforts, analyzing their role, influence, and effectiveness in mitigating the crisis.

Cuba's External Debt and Its Effect on Foreign Direct Investment

Foreign direct investment is essential for economic growth and development. We will examine how Cuba's external debt crisis has impacted foreign direct investment, exploring the challenges faced by investors and the measures taken by the government to attract and retain investment.

The Impact of Cuba's External Debt on Domestic Inflation and Currency Stability

The external debt crisis can have significant consequences for domestic inflation and currency stability. We will analyze the relationship between Cuba's external debt and these macroeconomic factors, shedding light on the challenges faced by the government in maintaining price stability and currency value.

Cuba's External Debt and Its Implications for the Country's Credit Rating

The credit rating of a country is crucial for accessing international financial markets and attracting investment. We will evaluate the impact of Cuba's external debt on its credit rating, examining the factors that influence credit rating agencies' assessments and the implications for the country's borrowing costs.

Analysis of Cuba's Debt Restructuring and Negotiation Processes with Creditors

Finally, we will analyze the debt restructuring and negotiation processes that Cuba has undertaken with its creditors. By examining the strategies employed, the outcomes achieved, and the lessons learned, we can identify potential solutions and best practices for future debt negotiations.

The Future Prospects for Cuba's External Debt and Potential Solutions for Long-term Sustainability

In the concluding section of this subchapter, we will explore the future prospects for Cuba's external debt and identify potential solutions for long-term debt sustainability. By considering the economic, political, and social dynamics at play, we can provide valuable insights and recommendations for bankers and policymakers alike.

Chapter 6: Cuban Government's Strategies for Managing External Debt and Delinquencies

Overview of Government Policies and Measures

In this subchapter, we will delve into the various government policies and measures that have been implemented by the Cuban government to address the country's external debt crisis. As bankers, it is crucial to understand the strategies and actions taken by the government in managing their debt and delinquencies, as this directly impacts our dealings with Cuba's external debt.

The history and causes of Cuba's external debt crisis are multifaceted and intertwined with the country's economic development. The Cuban government has taken several measures to address this crisis, including implementing austerity measures, increasing exports, and attracting foreign investment. These policies aim to generate revenue and stabilize the economy, ultimately reducing the burden of external debt.

One of the key strategies employed by the government is debt refinancing. The Cuban government has actively engaged with international financial institutions, such as the International Monetary Fund and World Bank, to negotiate favorable terms for debt repayment. These negotiations have resulted in debt restructuring, allowing Cuba to manage its debt obligations more effectively.

Additionally, the Cuban government has implemented measures to attract foreign direct investment (FDI). By offering incentives and creating favorable conditions for investment, the government aims to diversify its revenue sources and stimulate economic growth. FDI plays a crucial role in supporting the country's efforts to manage its external debt and enhance its economic development.

However, it is essential to consider the implications of Cuba's external debt on social welfare and public services. As the government allocates funds to debt repayment, there may be limited resources available for social programs and public services. This can potentially impact the well-being of the population and hinder the overall development of the country.

Furthermore, Cuba's external debt crisis can have implications for the country's credit rating. A high level of debt and delinquencies can negatively affect the country's creditworthiness, making it more challenging to access favorable financing in the future. Therefore, it is crucial for the government to carefully manage its debt and work towards improving its credit rating.

In conclusion, this subchapter provides an overview of the government policies and measures implemented by Cuba to address its external debt crisis. By understanding these strategies, bankers can gain insights into the country's financial situation and make informed decisions regarding Cuba's external debt. The future prospects for Cuba's external debt and potential solutions for long-term sustainability will also be discussed, allowing bankers to evaluate the risks and opportunities associated with Cuba's debt.

Debt Management Strategies Implemented by the Cuban Government

In the face of mounting external debt, the Cuban government has implemented a series of strategies aimed at managing its financial obligations and mitigating the impact on its economy. These strategies have been pivotal in navigating Cuba's external debt crisis and charting a path towards long-term sustainability. This subchapter will delve into the various debt management strategies adopted by the Cuban government, shedding light on their effectiveness and implications.

One of the key strategies employed by the Cuban government is debt refinancing. By renegotiating the terms of its existing debt, Cuba has been able to extend repayment periods, obtain lower interest rates, and secure more favorable conditions. This has provided the government with much-needed breathing space to address its economic challenges and stimulate growth. Additionally, debt refinancing has allowed Cuba to improve its credit rating, making it more attractive to foreign investors and facilitating access to international financial markets.

Another crucial aspect of the Cuban government's debt management strategy is the restructuring and negotiation processes with creditors. Through these processes, Cuba has sought to reduce the overall burden of its debt by reaching agreements that entail partial debt forgiveness, debt swaps, or debt rescheduling. These measures have provided significant relief, allowing the government to redirect resources towards social welfare programs and public services, thus improving the quality of life for its citizens.

Furthermore, the Cuban government has actively engaged with international financial institutions to secure support for its debt refinancing efforts. By collaborating with organizations such as the International Monetary Fund and the World Bank, Cuba has been able to access financial assistance, technical expertise, and policy advice. This partnership has been instrumental in bolstering the country's debt management capabilities and fostering economic stability.

Looking ahead, the future prospects for Cuba's external debt remain uncertain. However, there are potential solutions for long-term sustainability. The Cuban government must continue to prioritize economic diversification, attracting foreign direct investment, and implementing structural reforms. These measures will not only help reduce reliance on external borrowing but also stimulate economic growth, enhance productivity, and improve the country's creditworthiness.

In conclusion, the Cuban government has implemented a range of debt management strategies to tackle its external debt crisis. Through debt refinancing, restructuring, and negotiation processes, Cuba has successfully alleviated the burden of debt and created opportunities for economic development. Collaboration with international financial institutions has played a pivotal role in supporting these efforts. As Cuba moves forward, it must remain committed to implementing sustainable economic policies and attracting investment to ensure the long-term sustainability of its external debt.

Evaluation of the Effectiveness of these Strategies

In order to fully understand the impact of Cuba's external debt crisis and the strategies implemented by the Cuban government to manage it, it is crucial to evaluate the effectiveness of these strategies. This evaluation will provide valuable insights for bankers and those interested in Cuba's external debt, delinquencies, and refinancing difficulties.

One of the key strategies employed by the Cuban government is debt restructuring and negotiation processes with creditors. This approach aims to alleviate the burden of debt while ensuring the country's ability to meet its financial obligations. By analyzing the outcomes of these processes, bankers can assess the effectiveness of such negotiations and their impact on Cuba's debt sustainability.

Additionally, the role of international financial institutions in Cuba's debt refinancing efforts should be evaluated. These institutions play a crucial role in providing financial support and guidance to countries facing debt crises. By examining the assistance provided by these institutions to Cuba and its impact on debt management, bankers can gain insights into the effectiveness of such collaborations.

Another important aspect to consider is the implications of Cuba's external debt on social welfare and public services. The effectiveness of the government's strategies can be evaluated by assessing their impact on the provision of essential services to the Cuban population. This evaluation will shed light on whether the strategies prioritize social welfare and public services, and if they are successful in maintaining a balance between debt management and the well-being of the citizens.

Furthermore, the effect of Cuba's external debt on foreign direct investment (FDI) and domestic inflation and currency stability should also be assessed. Bankers need to understand how Cuba's debt crisis influences the country's attractiveness to foreign investors and its ability to maintain a stable economic environment. This evaluation will provide insights into the effectiveness of the strategies in attracting FDI and ensuring economic stability.

Lastly, the implications of Cuba's external debt on the country's credit rating and the future prospects for long-term sustainability should be analyzed. Bankers need to assess the impact of the debt crisis on Cuba's creditworthiness and the potential consequences for future borrowing. By evaluating the effectiveness of the strategies in improving the country's credit rating and ensuring long-term sustainability, bankers can make informed decisions regarding financial transactions with Cuba.

In conclusion, evaluating the effectiveness of the strategies employed by the Cuban government to manage external debt and delinquencies is crucial for bankers and those interested in Cuba's debt crisis. By analyzing the outcomes of debt restructuring and negotiation processes, assessing the role of international financial institutions, and evaluating the impact on social welfare, FDI, inflation, and credit rating, bankers can gain a comprehensive understanding of the effectiveness of these strategies and their implications for long-term sustainability.

Chapter 7: Implications on Social Welfare and Public Services

Impact of Cuba's External Debt Crisis on Social Welfare Programs

The Impact of Cuba's External Debt Crisis on Social Welfare Programs

As bankers, it is crucial for us to understand the implications of Cuba's external debt crisis on various aspects of the country's economy and society. One area that is significantly affected is the social welfare programs that the Cuban government has put in place to ensure the well-being of its citizens. In this subchapter, we will delve into the impact of the debt crisis on these programs and the potential consequences for the people of Cuba.

Cuba's external debt, delinquencies, and refinancing difficulties have created significant challenges for the government in maintaining its social welfare programs. With limited resources available, the government has been forced to make difficult decisions regarding the allocation of funds. As a result, social welfare programs such as healthcare, education, and housing have faced budget cuts, leading to a decline in the quality and accessibility of these services.

The history and causes of Cuba's external debt crisis play a crucial role in understanding the current situation. Years of economic mismanagement, reliance on imports, and external shocks have contributed to the accumulation of debt. The Cuban government's strategies for managing external debt and delinquencies have not been sufficient to address the root causes of the crisis, exacerbating the impact on social welfare programs.

The implications of Cuba's external debt on social welfare and public services are dire. The healthcare system, once renowned for its quality and accessibility, has suffered from a lack of resources, resulting in a decline in the quality of care and limited access to necessary medications and treatments. Similarly, the education system has faced challenges in maintaining adequate infrastructure and providing quality education to all Cuban children. Housing programs have also been affected, with a shortage of affordable housing and deteriorating living conditions.

The role of international financial institutions in Cuba's debt refinancing efforts cannot be overlooked. Their involvement and support are crucial in helping the country restructure its debt and find sustainable solutions. However, it is essential to ensure that the terms and conditions imposed by these institutions do not further burden the Cuban people or hinder their access to social welfare programs.

Furthermore, Cuba's external debt crisis has had a significant impact on foreign direct investment (FDI) in the country. Investors are often reluctant to invest in a country with a high level of debt and economic instability. This, in turn, hampers economic development and has a direct impact on social welfare programs.

The debt crisis also poses challenges for domestic inflation and currency stability. The government's efforts to address the debt crisis, such as devaluing the currency, can lead to higher inflation rates, making it even more challenging for the average Cuban citizen to afford basic necessities.

Additionally, Cuba's external debt has implications for the country's credit rating, which affects its ability to borrow in the future. A low credit rating can hinder economic growth and further limit the government's ability to fund social welfare programs adequately.

In conclusion, the impact of Cuba's external debt crisis on social welfare programs is severe and far-reaching. The decline in the quality and accessibility of healthcare, education, and housing has had a detrimental effect on the well-being of Cuban citizens. It is crucial for bankers and policymakers to understand these implications and work towards finding long-term sustainable solutions that prioritize the needs of the Cuban people while addressing the country's external debt crisis.

Effects on Public Services, Education, and Healthcare

Cuba's external debt crisis has had significant implications for the country's public services, education, and healthcare systems. As bankers and individuals concerned with economic development, it is crucial to understand the impact of this crisis on social welfare and the well-being of the Cuban population.

One of the most immediate effects of the external debt crisis is the strain it places on public services. With limited financial resources available, the Cuban government has been forced to allocate a significant portion of its budget towards servicing its debt, leaving fewer funds available for essential public services such as transportation, infrastructure, and social programs. This has resulted in a deterioration of public services, causing inconvenience and hardships for the Cuban people.

Another area greatly affected by the debt crisis is education. Historically, Cuba has placed great importance on its education system, which has been a cornerstone of its social development. However, the debt crisis has taken a toll on this sector, leading to reduced funding for schools, universities, and educational programs. This has resulted in a decline in the quality of education, limiting opportunities for Cuban students and hindering the country's human capital development.

Similarly, healthcare has suffered as a consequence of the external debt crisis. Cuba has long been recognized for its robust healthcare system, which provides free and accessible medical services to its citizens. However, limited financial resources due to the debt crisis have resulted in a shortage of medical supplies, reduced access to quality healthcare facilities, and a strain on healthcare professionals. This has had a detrimental impact on the overall health and well-being of the Cuban population.

It is important to note that the implications of Cuba's external debt crisis on public services, education, and healthcare extend beyond the immediate effects. The long-term consequences include a decrease in foreign direct investment due to the country's unstable financial situation, an increase in domestic inflation, and a decline in the country's credit rating. These factors further exacerbate the challenges faced by the Cuban government in managing its debt and finding sustainable solutions.

To address these issues, the Cuban government has implemented strategies to manage external debt and delinquencies, including debt restructuring and negotiation processes with creditors. Additionally, the role of international financial institutions in assisting Cuba with debt refinancing efforts cannot be overlooked. However, a comprehensive analysis of Cuba's debt history, causes, and potential long-term solutions is necessary to ensure the future prospects for the country's external debt and its impact on public services, education, and healthcare.

Case Studies: How Social Welfare and Public Services Were Affected

In this subchapter, we will delve into the case studies that demonstrate the profound impact of Cuba's external debt crisis on social welfare and public services. As bankers, understanding the consequences of this crisis is crucial for assessing the country's financial stability and potential solutions for long-term sustainability.

One significant case study revolves around Cuba's healthcare system. Historically, Cuba has been renowned for its robust healthcare infrastructure, providing free healthcare services to all its citizens. However, the external debt crisis has severely strained the healthcare sector, resulting in a decline in the quality and availability of medical services. Hospitals are grappling with shortages of essential supplies, outdated equipment, and a lack of skilled healthcare professionals due to inadequate funding.

Another case study focuses on education. Cuba's commitment to education has been commendable, with high literacy rates and a well-developed educational system. However, the external debt crisis has hindered the government's ability to allocate sufficient resources to education. As a result, schools face deteriorating infrastructure, overcrowded classrooms, and a scarcity of teaching materials, impeding the quality of education provided to Cuban students.

Additionally, the crisis has taken a toll on the country's social welfare programs. Cuba's social welfare system has traditionally provided support to vulnerable populations, including the elderly, disabled, and low-income families. However, budget constraints caused by the debt crisis have forced the government to reduce social welfare benefits, exacerbating poverty and inequality within the country.

It is essential to recognize the interconnectedness between social welfare, public services, and economic development. The decline in social welfare and public services has hindered Cuba's economic growth potential, as a healthy and educated population is pivotal for long-term economic prosperity.

As the Cuban government grapples with external debt and delinquencies, it is imperative for international financial institutions to play a supportive role. By providing refinancing options and debt restructuring solutions, these institutions can alleviate the burden on Cuba's economy and help safeguard social welfare and public services. Moreover, attracting foreign direct investment becomes increasingly challenging amidst a debt crisis, further highlighting the need for external assistance.

By analyzing these case studies, bankers can gain valuable insights into the implications of Cuba's external debt crisis on social welfare and public services. This understanding will not only aid in assessing the country's credit rating and inflationary pressures but also contribute to the formulation of effective strategies for debt management and long-term sustainability. Ultimately, achieving a balance between debt servicing and investment in social welfare is crucial for Cuba's future prospects and economic stability.

Chapter 8: Role of International Financial Institutions

Involvement of International Financial Institutions in Cuba's Debt Refinancing Efforts

The involvement of international financial institutions in Cuba's debt refinancing efforts has played a crucial role in addressing the country's external debt crisis. This subchapter aims to shed light on the significance of these institutions and their contributions to Cuba's ongoing struggle for economic stability and sustainable development.

International financial institutions, such as the International Monetary Fund (IMF), World Bank, and Inter-American Development Bank (IDB), have been actively engaged in Cuba's debt refinancing efforts. These institutions have recognized the urgent need to support the Cuban government in managing its external debt and delinquencies, given their potential impact on the country's economic development.

The IMF, in particular, has been instrumental in providing technical assistance and policy advice to Cuba. Through its debt sustainability analysis, the IMF has helped the Cuban government assess the sustainability of its external debt and develop strategies for debt management. The IMF has also facilitated negotiations between Cuba and its creditors, advocating for debt restructuring and debt relief measures to alleviate the burden on the country's economy.

Similarly, the World Bank and IDB have offered financial support to Cuba through their lending programs and development projects. These institutions have recognized the importance of addressing Cuba's external debt crisis as a means to promote economic growth, poverty reduction, and social welfare in the country. By providing financial resources and technical expertise, the World Bank and IDB have enabled

Cuba to undertake critical reforms and investments in key sectors such as infrastructure, education, and healthcare.

The involvement of international financial institutions in Cuba's debt refinancing efforts has also had implications for the country's credit rating and foreign direct investment (FDI) prospects. By assisting Cuba in managing its external debt and implementing structural reforms, these institutions have helped improve the country's creditworthiness and attract FDI. As a result, Cuba has been able to access international capital markets at more favorable terms, which has enhanced its ability to finance development projects and stimulate economic growth.

Looking forward, the future prospects for Cuba's external debt largely depend on the country's ability to implement comprehensive economic reforms, attract foreign investment, and diversify its sources of revenue. International financial institutions will continue to play a crucial role in supporting Cuba's debt refinancing efforts and promoting long-term sustainability. By continuing to provide technical assistance, policy advice, and financial resources, these institutions can contribute to the country's economic recovery and pave the way for a brighter future.

Analysis of IMF, World Bank, and Other Institutions' Roles

The role of international financial institutions, such as the International Monetary Fund (IMF) and the World Bank, is of great significance when it comes to understanding and addressing Cuba's external debt crisis. In this subchapter, we will delve into the analysis of these institutions' roles and their impact on the country's debt refinancing efforts.

The IMF and the World Bank have been instrumental in providing financial assistance and expertise to countries facing economic challenges, including debt crises. Cuba, with its mounting external debt and delinquencies, has sought the support and guidance of these institutions in managing its debt burden and finding solutions for long-term sustainability.

One of the key roles played by the IMF is providing financial aid packages to countries in need, often contingent on implementing economic reforms. These reforms may include fiscal austerity measures, structural adjustments, and liberalization of markets. Cuba, however, has been hesitant to adopt these measures due to its socialist economic system. As a result, the IMF's role in Cuba's debt refinancing efforts has been limited.

The World Bank, on the other hand, has focused on providing technical assistance and development projects to countries, including Cuba, to improve their economic and social conditions. While the World Bank has not provided direct financial assistance to Cuba due to its outstanding external debt, it has played a crucial role in advising and supporting the country in areas such as poverty reduction, infrastructure development, and sustainable growth.

In addition to the IMF and the World Bank, other international institutions, such as regional development banks and creditor committees, have also been involved in Cuba's debt restructuring and negotiation processes. These institutions have worked closely with the Cuban government and creditors to find mutually beneficial solutions, often involving debt forgiveness, rescheduling, or refinancing.

The implications of Cuba's external debt on the country's credit rating, foreign direct investment, inflation, and currency stability cannot be overlooked. The high debt burden and delinquencies have hindered Cuba's ability to attract foreign investment and maintain stable economic conditions. Furthermore, the country's credit rating has been downgraded, making it more difficult and expensive for Cuba to borrow on international financial markets.

Looking towards the future, the prospects for Cuba's external debt remain uncertain. However, potential solutions for long-term sustainability include diversifying the economy, attracting foreign investment through policy reforms, and exploring debt relief options through negotiations with creditors and international financial institutions.

In conclusion, the analysis of the roles of the IMF, World Bank, and other international financial institutions is crucial in understanding and addressing Cuba's external debt crisis. While these institutions have provided support and guidance to the country, their effectiveness has been limited due to Cuba's unique economic and political circumstances. Moving forward, it will be essential for Cuba to explore innovative solutions and engage in constructive dialogue with creditors and international partners to ensure long-term sustainability and economic development.

Evaluation of the Impact of International Financial Institutions' Interventions

In the subchapter titled "Evaluation of the Impact of International Financial Institutions' Interventions," we will analyze the role of these institutions in addressing Cuba's external debt crisis. This evaluation is crucial for bankers and individuals interested in understanding the implications of international financial institutions' interventions on Cuba's economic development, social welfare, credit rating, and long-term sustainability.

International financial institutions, such as the International Monetary Fund (IMF) and the World Bank, play a significant role in assisting countries facing financial challenges. Their interventions in Cuba's external debt crisis have had both positive and negative impacts.

These institutions have provided financial assistance and expertise to help Cuba manage its external debt and delinquencies. Through debt refinancing efforts, the IMF and the World Bank have allowed Cuba to restructure its debt payments, providing the government with breathing space to focus on economic development and social welfare.

However, the impact of these interventions on Cuba's economic development has been mixed. While the refinancing efforts have provided short-term relief, the long-term sustainability of Cuba's external debt remains a concern. The country's high debt burden has limited its ability to attract foreign direct investment, hindering economic growth and diversification.

Furthermore, the interventions of international financial institutions have had implications for social welfare and public services in Cuba. The government has had to allocate a significant portion of its budget towards debt servicing, resulting in limited resources for social programs and infrastructure development. This has affected the overall well-being of the Cuban population.

In addition to economic and social impacts, the interventions of international financial institutions have influenced Cuba's credit rating and currency stability. The country's high external debt has had a negative effect on its creditworthiness, making it more difficult to access international capital markets. The debt burden has also put pressure on the Cuban currency, leading to potential inflation and currency instability.

To address these challenges, Cuba has engaged in debt restructuring and negotiation processes with its creditors. This analysis will delve into the effectiveness of these strategies and the outcomes achieved thus far.

Looking towards the future, this subchapter will explore potential solutions for long-term debt sustainability in Cuba. It will consider the importance of economic reforms, diversification of revenue sources, and the need for continued support from international financial institutions.

Overall, the evaluation of the impact of international financial institutions' interventions is crucial for bankers and individuals interested in Cuba's external debt crisis. It sheds light on the complex relationship between Cuba, international financial institutions, and the implications for economic development, social welfare, credit rating, and long-term sustainability.

Chapter 9: Effect on Foreign Direct Investment

Relationship between Cuba's External Debt and Foreign Direct Investment

Foreign direct investment (FDI) plays a crucial role in shaping Cuba's external debt landscape. This subchapter will delve into the intricate relationship between Cuba's external debt and FDI, highlighting the impact it has on the country's economic development, credit rating, inflation, and currency stability.

Cuba's external debt crisis has been a stumbling block for attracting FDI. Potential investors are cautious about investing in a country burdened by a high level of debt as it raises concerns about the government's ability to repay and the overall stability of the economy. The country's external debt acts as a deterrent for FDI, impeding its potential to stimulate economic growth and development.

The Cuban government recognizes the need to address its external debt crisis to attract FDI. To manage external debt and delinquencies, the government has implemented strategies such as debt refinancing and negotiation processes with creditors. These efforts aim to alleviate the burden of debt and create a more conducive environment for FDI inflows.

The implications of Cuba's external debt on social welfare and public services cannot be overlooked. High debt levels often result in reduced government spending on social programs, healthcare, and education. This, in turn, affects the overall well-being of the population and hampers the country's ability to provide quality public services.

International financial institutions also play a significant role in Cuba's debt refinancing efforts. Cooperation with these institutions can provide Cuba with access to financial resources and expertise, facilitating the management of its external debt and increasing its chances of attracting FDI.

Furthermore, Cuba's external debt has a direct impact on domestic inflation and currency stability. Excessive external debt can lead to inflationary pressures as the government may resort to printing more money to meet its debt obligations. This can result in a devaluation of the currency and further deter FDI inflows.

The country's external debt also has implications for its credit rating. A high level of debt relative to its GDP can lead to downgrades in credit ratings, making it more expensive for the government to borrow and limiting its access to international capital markets. This, in turn, affects the country's ability to attract FDI.

Analyzing Cuba's debt restructuring and negotiation processes with creditors provides valuable insights into the country's efforts to address its external debt crisis. Understanding these processes can shed light on the challenges faced by Cuba and potential solutions for long-term sustainability.

Looking ahead, the future prospects for Cuba's external debt are uncertain. However, adopting sustainable policies, promoting economic diversification, and attracting FDI can contribute to the country's long-term debt sustainability. This subchapter will provide an analysis of potential solutions and offer recommendations for policymakers and bankers to navigate Cuba's external debt challenges effectively.

Challenges Faced by Foreign Investors in the Context of Debt Crisis

In the complex landscape of Cuba's external debt crisis, foreign investors face a multitude of challenges that require careful consideration and strategic decision-making. Understanding these challenges is crucial for bankers seeking to navigate the intricacies of Cuba's economic environment and make informed investment decisions.

One of the primary challenges faced by foreign investors is the delinquencies and refinancing difficulties that arise from Cuba's external debt. The country has a long history of missed payments and struggles to meet its financial obligations, leading to a climate of uncertainty and risk for investors. This uncertainty is further compounded by the lack of transparency and reliable financial data provided by the Cuban government, making it difficult for investors to accurately assess the country's creditworthiness.

Cuba's external debt also has a significant impact on the country's economic development. High levels of debt restrict the government's ability to invest in infrastructure, education, and public services, which in turn hinders economic growth and potential returns for investors. Additionally, the burden of debt servicing often leads to austerity measures and budget cuts, further impeding the development of key sectors and creating potential challenges for foreign investors.

The Cuban government's strategies for managing external debt and delinquencies pose another challenge for foreign investors. These strategies often involve debt restructuring and negotiation processes with creditors, which can result in unfavorable terms for investors. Moreover, the government's reliance on short-term debt refinancing increases the risk of default and adds additional uncertainty to the investment landscape.

The role of international financial institutions in Cuba's debt refinancing efforts is also a crucial factor for foreign investors to consider. The involvement of institutions such as the International Monetary Fund and the World Bank can influence the terms of debt restructuring and the overall investment climate. Understanding the dynamics between the

Cuban government and these institutions is essential for bankers seeking to assess the risk and potential returns of their investments.

Furthermore, Cuba's external debt has implications for other aspects of the country's economy, such as foreign direct investment, inflation, currency stability, and credit ratings. These factors can directly impact the profitability and sustainability of foreign investments, making them critical considerations for bankers.

In conclusion, foreign investors in Cuba's debt crisis face numerous challenges, from delinquencies and refinancing difficulties to the impact on economic development and the role of international financial institutions. It is imperative for bankers to thoroughly analyze these challenges and their potential implications in order to make informed investment decisions. By understanding the history and causes of Cuba's external debt crisis, as well as the government's strategies and potential solutions, bankers can navigate these challenges and identify opportunities for long-term sustainability in Cuba's investment landscape.

Case Studies: How External Debt Influenced Foreign Direct Investment

In the ever-changing landscape of international finance, one cannot underestimate the interplay between external debt and foreign direct investment (FDI). This subchapter aims to provide bankers with a comprehensive understanding of how Cuba's external debt crisis has influenced FDI, exploring its historical causes, implications, and potential solutions for long-term sustainability.

Cuba's External Debt, Delinquencies, and Refinancing Difficulties form the foundation of this analysis. By examining the history and causes of Cuba's external debt crisis, bankers gain valuable insights into the factors that have contributed to the country's current financial situation. Understanding the Cuban government's strategies for managing external debt and delinquencies is crucial in comprehending the challenges they face and the potential solutions they seek.

Moreover, this subchapter delves into the implications of Cuba's external debt on economic development, social welfare, and public services. By exploring the impact on domestic inflation and currency stability, bankers can better assess the risks associated with investing in Cuba. Additionally, the implications for the country's credit rating are examined, shedding light on the potential consequences of the debt crisis on Cuba's financial reputation.

International financial institutions play a vital role in Cuba's debt refinancing efforts, and their involvement is analyzed in this subchapter. By understanding the mechanisms and strategies employed in debt restructuring and negotiation processes with creditors, bankers can gain valuable insights into potential future scenarios and the associated risks.

Furthermore, this subchapter investigates the impact of Cuba's external debt on FDI. By examining case studies and real-world examples, bankers can gauge how this debt crisis has affected the willingness of foreign investors to enter the Cuban market. This analysis includes an assessment of the country's credit rating, economic stability, and long-term sustainability, providing bankers with a comprehensive understanding of the risks and rewards associated with FDI in Cuba.

Finally, this subchapter concludes by exploring the future prospects for Cuba's external debt and proposing potential solutions for long-term sustainability. By considering the lessons learned from the past, bankers can identify strategies that may mitigate the risk of future debt crises and create a more favorable environment for FDI in Cuba.

In conclusion, this subchapter provides bankers with a holistic view of how external debt has influenced foreign direct investment in Cuba. By examining case studies, historical causes, and potential solutions, this analysis equips bankers with the knowledge necessary to navigate the complexities of Cuba's external debt crisis and make informed decisions regarding FDI.

Chapter 10: Impact on Domestic Inflation and Currency Stability

Analysis of the Relationship between Debt Crisis and Inflation

In this subchapter, we will delve into the intricate relationship between debt crisis and inflation in the context of Cuba's external debt. As bankers, it is crucial for us to understand how these two factors interact and influence each other, as they have significant implications for economic stability and development.

Cuba's External Debt, Delinquencies, and Refinancing Difficulties

Firstly, we will examine the magnitude of Cuba's external debt and the challenges it faces in terms of delinquencies and refinancing. By analyzing the historical data and trends, we can gain insights into the root causes of the debt crisis and identify patterns that may help us formulate effective solutions.

Cuba's External Debt and its Impact on Economic Development

Next, we will explore the impact of Cuba's external debt on its economic development. By examining case studies and empirical evidence, we will assess how the debt burden hinders economic growth, investment, and productivity in various sectors. This analysis will provide valuable insights into the factors that need to be addressed for sustainable economic development.

The Impact of Cuba's External Debt on Domestic Inflation and Currency Stability

Furthermore, we will analyze the direct correlation between Cuba's external debt and domestic inflation. By examining the historical relationship between these two factors, we can determine the extent to which debt crisis contributes to inflationary pressures and currency instability. This understanding will enable us to devise strategies to mitigate these adverse effects.

Cuba's External Debt and its Implications for the Country's Credit Rating

Additionally, we will discuss the implications of Cuba's external debt on its credit rating. By examining how the debt crisis affects the perception of risk among international creditors and credit rating agencies, we can evaluate the long-term consequences for Cuba's access to international capital markets.

Analysis of Cuba's Debt Restructuring and Negotiation Processes with Creditors

Furthermore, we will analyze Cuba's debt restructuring and negotiation processes with creditors. By examining past experiences and successful cases, we can identify best practices and lessons learned that can guide future debt negotiations, ensuring more favorable outcomes for both Cuba and its creditors.

The Future Prospects for Cuba's External Debt and Potential Solutions for Long-Term Sustainability

Finally, we will assess the future prospects for Cuba's external debt and explore potential solutions for long-term sustainability. By considering various scenarios and policy options, we can provide informed recommendations to mitigate the debt crisis and establish a sustainable path for Cuba's economy.

In conclusion, the analysis of the relationship between debt crisis and inflation in the context of Cuba's external debt is crucial for bankers seeking to understand the complexities of this issue. By examining historical data, economic indicators, and case studies, we can gain valuable insights into the causes, implications, and potential solutions for Cuba's external debt crisis. This knowledge will enable us to make informed decisions and provide effective financial advice to our clients.

Effects of Debt Crisis on Currency Stability

Currency stability is a crucial factor in any country's economic development, and the impact of a debt crisis on currency stability cannot be overstated. In the context of Cuba's external debt crisis, the effects on currency stability have been profound and far-reaching.

One of the primary effects of the debt crisis on currency stability is the depreciation of the Cuban peso. As the country struggles to meet its debt obligations, the value of the currency has plummeted. This depreciation has severe consequences for both domestic and international trade, as it makes imports more expensive and reduces the purchasing power of the Cuban population.

Furthermore, the debt crisis has also led to increased inflationary pressures in the country. As the government prints more money to fund its debt repayments, the supply of money in the economy increases, leading to higher prices for goods and services. This inflation erodes the value of the currency even further, exacerbating the currency stability problem.

The debt crisis has also had implications for Cuba's credit rating. As the country defaults on its debt payments and struggles to refinance its obligations, international credit rating agencies have downgraded Cuba's creditworthiness. This downgrade not only increases borrowing costs for the country but also undermines investor confidence, leading to a further decline in currency stability.

In addition, the debt crisis has had a significant impact on foreign direct investment (FDI) in Cuba. As investors become wary of the country's financial instability, they are less willing to invest in Cuban businesses.

This lack of FDI reduces capital inflows, further weakening the currency and making it more vulnerable to external shocks.

To manage the debt crisis and mitigate its effects on currency stability, the Cuban government has employed various strategies. These include debt restructuring and negotiation processes with creditors, seeking assistance from international financial institutions, and implementing austerity measures to reduce spending and increase revenue.

Looking ahead, the future prospects for Cuba's external debt remain uncertain. However, potential solutions for long-term sustainability include implementing structural reforms to boost economic growth, diversifying the country's export base, and attracting foreign investment in sectors with high growth potential.

In conclusion, the debt crisis in Cuba has had a detrimental effect on currency stability, leading to a depreciation of the Cuban peso, increased inflation, and a decline in the country's credit rating. These effects have further hampered economic development and foreign direct investment. However, with the implementation of appropriate measures and reforms, there is hope for long-term sustainability and the restoration of currency stability in Cuba.

Case Studies: Inflation and Currency Stability in the Context of Cuba's External Debt Crisis

In the complex landscape of Cuba's external debt crisis, one cannot deny the profound impact it has had on the country's economic development, social welfare, and public services. Among the multitude of challenges faced by the Cuban government, inflation and currency stability have emerged as critical concerns that demand careful analysis and consideration.

The history and causes of Cuba's external debt crisis are deeply intertwined with the country's economic policies, international relationships, and financial mismanagement. As bankers seeking to understand the intricacies of this crisis, it is essential to examine case studies that shed light on the relationship between external debt and its impact on inflation and currency stability.

One such case study is the period of debt refinancing difficulties and delinquencies experienced by the Cuban government. As external debt piled up, the government struggled to meet its financial obligations, resulting in a severe strain on the economy. These difficulties led to a significant depreciation of the Cuban peso, triggering rampant inflation and currency instability. Understanding the root causes of this phenomenon is crucial for devising effective strategies to mitigate its effects.

Moreover, the role of international financial institutions in Cuba's debt refinancing efforts cannot be overlooked. These institutions play a critical role in determining the terms and conditions of debt restructuring, which directly impacts inflation and currency stability. Analyzing the negotiation processes between Cuba and its creditors provides valuable insights into the challenges faced by the country and the potential solutions that can be explored.

The impact of Cuba's external debt on domestic inflation and currency stability is not limited to economic factors alone. It has far-reaching implications for social welfare and public services. As inflation erodes the purchasing power of the population, access to essential goods and services becomes increasingly challenging. This, in turn, fuels social discontent and exacerbates existing social inequalities.

Furthermore, Cuba's external debt crisis has implications for the country's credit rating, which has a direct impact on its ability to attract foreign direct investment. Investors are wary of countries with high levels of debt and unstable currencies, making it crucial for bankers to understand the link between external debt and its effect on foreign direct investment.

Considering the long-term sustainability of Cuba's external debt, it is imperative to analyze potential solutions and future prospects. Examining successful debt restructuring models implemented by other countries can provide valuable insights for the Cuban government. Exploring alternative sources of financing and prioritizing economic reforms can also contribute to long-term sustainability and alleviate the burden on inflation and currency stability.

In conclusion, the case studies of inflation and currency stability in the context of Cuba's external debt crisis offer valuable lessons for bankers and policymakers. By understanding the historical causes, analyzing negotiation processes, and exploring potential solutions, it becomes possible to navigate the complexities of this crisis and work towards a sustainable future for Cuba.

Chapter 11: Implications for Credit Rating

Importance of Credit Rating in the Context of External Debt Crisis

In the complex world of international finance, credit rating plays a crucial role in determining a country's financial stability and its ability to manage external debt. This subchapter will shed light on the importance of credit rating in the context of Cuba's external debt crisis, offering valuable insights for bankers and anyone interested in understanding the intricacies of this ongoing issue.

A credit rating is an assessment of a country's creditworthiness, indicating its ability to repay debt obligations. In the case of Cuba, which has been grappling with a severe external debt crisis, a credit rating assumes even more significance. A country's credit rating influences its access to international financial markets and its ability to obtain loans at favorable interest rates. A high credit rating can attract foreign investors and foster economic growth, while a low credit rating can deter potential investors and exacerbate the debt crisis.

Cuba's external debt, delinquencies, and refinancing difficulties have had a profound impact on its economic development. A poor credit rating can hinder the country's efforts to refinance its debt and address its delinquencies effectively. By evaluating Cuba's creditworthiness, credit rating agencies provide valuable information to bankers and investors, helping them make informed decisions about lending and investment opportunities in the country.

The history and causes of Cuba's external debt crisis are intricately linked to its credit rating. Understanding the factors that have contributed to the crisis is crucial for bankers seeking to navigate the complex landscape of Cuba's external debt. It is imperative for the Cuban government to adopt effective strategies for managing external debt and delinquencies to improve its credit rating and restore investor confidence.

Furthermore, the implications of Cuba's external debt on social welfare and public services cannot be overlooked. A country burdened with high levels of external debt may struggle to allocate sufficient resources to crucial sectors such as healthcare, education, and infrastructure development. Bankers must be aware of these implications when assessing the country's creditworthiness and potential investment opportunities.

International financial institutions also play a pivotal role in Cuba's debt refinancing efforts. Their involvement can help stabilize the country's financial situation and improve its credit rating. Bankers need to closely monitor the role and actions of these institutions to gauge the potential impact on Cuba's external debt crisis.

Cuba's external debt crisis also has a significant effect on foreign direct investment (FDI). A poor credit rating can deter foreign investors, impeding the country's economic growth and development. Bankers need to consider the impact of Cuba's external debt on FDI when evaluating investment prospects.

Additionally, the impact of Cuba's external debt on domestic inflation and currency stability cannot be ignored. High levels of debt can lead to inflationary pressures and currency depreciation, adversely affecting the country's economic stability. Bankers must carefully analyze these factors when assessing the risk associated with lending or investing in Cuba.

Cuba's external debt crisis also has implications for the country's credit rating. A lower credit rating can further exacerbate the debt crisis, creating a vicious cycle that becomes difficult to break. Bankers must consider the potential impact on Cuba's credit rating when evaluating the country's debt restructuring and negotiation processes with creditors.

Looking towards the future, understanding the long-term sustainability of Cuba's external debt is of utmost importance. Bankers need to explore potential solutions and strategies to ensure the country's debt remains manageable and sustainable in the long run. This subchapter will delve into the possibilities and challenges ahead, offering valuable insights for bankers seeking a comprehensive understanding of Cuba's external debt crisis and its implications for the country's credit rating.

In conclusion, the importance of credit rating in the context of Cuba's external debt crisis cannot be overstated. Bankers must recognize the pivotal role that credit rating plays in determining a country's financial stability, access to international financial markets, and potential for economic growth. This subchapter will provide a comprehensive analysis of the significance of credit rating in the context of Cuba's external debt crisis, offering valuable insights and guidance for bankers navigating this complex issue.

Evaluation of Cuba's Credit Rating in Light of the Debt Crisis

Cuba's external debt crisis has had significant implications for the country's credit rating, creating a challenging environment that requires a thorough evaluation. This subchapter aims to provide a comprehensive analysis of Cuba's credit rating in light of the debt crisis, offering insights and recommendations from a banker's perspective.

Cuba's external debt, delinquencies, and refinancing difficulties have had a profound impact on its credit rating. The country's history of defaulting on debt payments has resulted in a loss of investor confidence and a downgrade in its creditworthiness. This, in turn, has made it increasingly difficult for Cuba to access new sources of financing and refinance its existing debt.

The Cuban government has employed various strategies to manage its external debt and delinquencies. These include debt restructuring, negotiation processes with creditors, and seeking assistance from international financial institutions. However, the effectiveness of these strategies in improving Cuba's credit rating remains a subject of debate.

The implications of Cuba's external debt on social welfare and public services cannot be ignored. As the country struggles to meet its debt obligations, it has faced significant challenges in providing adequate healthcare, education, and infrastructure development. This has resulted in a decline in the overall well-being of its citizens.

The role of international financial institutions in Cuba's debt refinancing efforts is crucial. These institutions can provide technical expertise, financial support, and guidance to help Cuba navigate its debt crisis. However, their involvement is often contingent on the country's commitment to implementing economic reforms and improving its creditworthiness.

Cuba's external debt also has implications for foreign direct investment (FDI). The high debt levels and credit rating downgrade have deterred potential investors, limiting the inflow of FDI into the country. This, in turn, hampers economic growth and development.

Moreover, the impact of Cuba's external debt on domestic inflation and currency stability is significant. The country's debt burden puts pressure on its currency, leading to depreciation and inflationary pressures. This further exacerbates the economic challenges faced by Cuba.

Analyzing Cuba's debt restructuring and negotiation processes with creditors is essential for understanding the country's current situation. By examining the successes and failures of these processes, valuable lessons can be learned and potential solutions identified.

Looking towards the future, addressing Cuba's external debt crisis and ensuring long-term sustainability is of paramount importance. Potential solutions include implementing comprehensive economic reforms, attracting foreign investment, diversifying the economy, and improving debt management practices.

In conclusion, evaluating Cuba's credit rating in light of the debt crisis is crucial for understanding the country's current economic challenges. This subchapter provides a comprehensive analysis of Cuba's external debt crisis from a banker's perspective, exploring its impact on various aspects such as economic development, social welfare, FDI, inflation, and currency stability. By examining the history, causes, and implications of Cuba's debt crisis, this chapter aims to provide valuable insights and potential solutions for long-term sustainability.

Effects on Investment Climate and Access to International Markets

The external debt crisis that Cuba has been facing has had significant effects on the investment climate and its access to international markets. This subchapter aims to shed light on these effects and provide insights for bankers who are interested in understanding the implications for their financial institutions.

One of the key consequences of Cuba's external debt crisis is the deterioration of its investment climate. High levels of debt and delinquencies have created uncertainty and reduced investor confidence in the country. This has made it more difficult for Cuba to attract foreign direct investment (FDI), which is crucial for economic development. The lack of FDI inflows has hindered the modernization of industries, infrastructure, and technology, further hampering Cuba's ability to compete in international markets.

Moreover, Cuba's external debt has had a direct impact on the country's access to international markets. The high debt burden and delinquencies have made it challenging for the government to secure favorable financing terms and access to capital. This limits Cuba's ability to engage in international trade and hampers its economic growth potential. Additionally, the country's credit rating has been negatively affected, making it more expensive for Cuba to borrow and increasing its risk premium.

The Cuban government has implemented various strategies to manage its external debt and delinquencies. These strategies include debt restructuring and negotiation processes with creditors. While these efforts have provided short-term relief, they have not addressed the root causes of the debt crisis or provided long-term solutions for sustainability.

The role of international financial institutions (IFIs) in Cuba's debt refinancing efforts is crucial. IFIs can provide technical expertise, financial support, and guidance to help Cuba navigate its debt challenges. Their involvement can help improve Cuba's creditworthiness, access to international markets, and overall investment climate.

Furthermore, Cuba's external debt crisis has implications for social welfare and public services. The government's limited resources have been diverted to debt servicing, compromising its ability to invest in education, healthcare, and other essential services. This has had a direct impact on the well-being of the Cuban population.

In conclusion, Cuba's external debt crisis has had far-reaching effects on the investment climate and access to international markets. It has hindered foreign direct investment, limited access to capital, and negatively impacted the country's credit rating. The Cuban government's strategies for managing debt and delinquencies have provided short-term relief but have not addressed the root causes. The involvement of international financial institutions is crucial for providing expertise and support. The debt crisis has also compromised social welfare and public services, affecting the overall well-being of the Cuban population. Addressing these challenges and finding long-term solutions for debt sustainability is essential for the future prospects of Cuba's external debt.

Chapter 12: Analysis of Debt Restructuring and Negotiation Processes

Overview of Cuba's Debt Restructuring Efforts

Cuba's external debt crisis has been a long-standing issue that has had significant implications for the country's economic development, social welfare, and public services. In this subchapter, we will delve into the history and causes of Cuba's external debt crisis, as well as the Cuban government's strategies for managing external debt and delinquencies. We will also explore the role of international financial institutions in Cuba's debt refinancing efforts and the implications of Cuba's external debt on various aspects of the country's economic landscape.

Cuba's external debt has been a result of various factors, including economic mismanagement, limited access to international financial markets, and geopolitical shifts. The country's debt crisis has hindered its economic development and has had a negative impact on social welfare and public services. The Cuban government has implemented various strategies to manage its debt, including debt rescheduling, debt forgiveness, and debt-for-equity swaps. These measures have aimed to reduce the burden of debt while ensuring the continuation of essential services for the Cuban people.

International financial institutions, such as the International Monetary Fund and the World Bank, have played a crucial role in Cuba's debt refinancing efforts. These institutions have provided financial assistance and technical expertise to help Cuba restructure its debt and negotiate with creditors. However, the involvement of these institutions has not been without challenges, as Cuba's political landscape and ideological differences have impacted the negotiation processes.

Cuba's external debt has also had implications for foreign direct investment in the country. High levels of debt and economic uncertainty have deterred potential investors, limiting Cuba's ability to attract much-needed foreign capital. Additionally, the country's debt crisis has had implications for domestic inflation and currency stability, as the government has had to implement austerity measures and currency devaluations to manage its debt.

The external debt crisis has also had implications for Cuba's credit rating, which has been downgraded by various credit rating agencies. This has further limited Cuba's ability to access international financial markets and has increased borrowing costs. Therefore, it is essential for Cuba to address its external debt crisis to regain investor confidence and improve its credit rating.

In conclusion, the subchapter provides an overview of Cuba's debt restructuring efforts and analyzes the impact of external debt on various aspects of the country's economy. It explores the history and causes of the debt crisis, the strategies employed by the Cuban government, and the role of international financial institutions. It also examines the implications of the debt crisis on social welfare, foreign direct investment, inflation, and credit rating. Finally, the subchapter discusses the future prospects for Cuba's external debt and potential solutions for long-term sustainability.

Analysis of Negotiation Processes with Creditors

When examining the history and causes of Cuba's external debt crisis, it is crucial to analyze the negotiation processes that have taken place between the Cuban government and its creditors. This subchapter aims to provide bankers with a comprehensive understanding of these negotiations and their implications.

Cuba's external debt has been a significant concern for both the government and the international financial community. The country has faced delinquencies and refinancing difficulties, leading to severe economic challenges and hampering its development. In order to address these issues, the Cuban government has employed various strategies to manage its external debt and delinquencies.

One key aspect to consider is the role of international financial institutions in assisting Cuba with its debt refinancing efforts. Organizations such as the International Monetary Fund and the World Bank have played a crucial role in providing financial support and guidance to the Cuban government. However, these institutions have also imposed strict conditions and requirements on the country, leading to complex negotiation processes.

The negotiation processes between Cuba and its creditors have had significant implications for social welfare and public services. As the government allocates a substantial portion of its budget to debt servicing, resources for healthcare, education, and infrastructure have been constrained. This has had a direct impact on the well-being of the Cuban population.

Furthermore, Cuba's external debt has also affected foreign direct investment and the country's credit rating. High debt levels and difficulties in debt management have discouraged potential investors, limiting economic growth. Additionally, the country's credit rating has been downgraded due to its high debt burden, further exacerbating its financial challenges.

Analyzing Cuba's debt restructuring processes is essential in understanding the country's negotiation strategies with creditors. The government has pursued various approaches, including debt-for-equity swaps and extending repayment terms. These negotiations have been complex, requiring careful consideration of economic, political, and social factors.

Looking ahead, it is crucial to consider the future prospects for Cuba's external debt and identify potential solutions for long-term sustainability. Sustainable debt management strategies, increased foreign investment, and economic reforms are crucial for alleviating the debt burden and promoting economic growth.

In conclusion, analyzing the negotiation processes with creditors is essential for understanding the causes and implications of Cuba's external debt crisis. Bankers must comprehend the strategies employed by the Cuban government, the role of international financial institutions, and the potential solutions for long-term sustainability. By gaining a comprehensive understanding of these processes, bankers can make informed decisions and contribute to the resolution of Cuba's debt challenges.

Lessons Learned from Cuba's Debt Restructuring Experience

As bankers, it is crucial for us to examine the lessons learned from Cuba's debt restructuring experience. By understanding the history and causes of Cuba's external debt crisis, we can gain valuable insights into the challenges faced by the Cuban government and the strategies they employed to manage their debt and delinquencies. These lessons can help shape our own approach to dealing with similar situations in the future.

Cuba's external debt has had a significant impact on its economic development. The high levels of debt and the difficulties in refinancing have hindered the country's ability to attract foreign direct investment and maintain currency stability. This has had implications for social welfare and public services, as limited resources have been diverted towards debt servicing instead.

One important lesson that emerges from Cuba's experience is the role of international financial institutions in debt refinancing efforts. The Cuban government had to rely on the support and negotiation skills of these institutions to secure favorable terms and alleviate the burden of their debt. This highlights the importance of building strong relationships with these institutions and leveraging their expertise in managing debt crises.

Furthermore, the Cuban government's strategies for managing external debt and delinquencies provide valuable insights. Their negotiation processes with creditors and debt restructuring efforts can serve as a blueprint for other countries struggling with similar challenges. By analyzing these strategies, we can identify best practices and potential pitfalls to be avoided.

Moving forward, it is crucial to consider the long-term sustainability of Cuba's external debt. The country's credit rating has been affected by its high debt levels, making it challenging to access affordable financing. Exploring potential solutions for long-term sustainability, such as debt forgiveness, debt-for-nature swaps, and diversification of funding sources, can help mitigate the negative impact on Cuba's credit rating.

In conclusion, the lessons learned from Cuba's debt restructuring experience are invaluable for bankers navigating the complex world of external debt. By understanding the history, causes, and strategies employed by the Cuban government, we can enhance our own approach to managing debt crises. Furthermore, exploring the implications of Cuba's debt on economic development, social welfare, inflation, and currency stability, as well as the role of international financial institutions, offers a comprehensive perspective on the challenges and potential solutions for long-term sustainability.

Chapter 13: Future Prospects and Potential Solutions

Forecasting Cuba's External Debt Sustainability

The subchapter "Forecasting Cuba's External Debt Sustainability" delves into the future prospects for Cuba's external debt and potential solutions for long-term sustainability. This section is specifically tailored to bankers who are interested in understanding the country's external debt crisis from a financial perspective.

In recent years, Cuba has faced significant challenges in managing its external debt, leading to delinquencies and refinancing difficulties. In order to analyze the future trajectory of Cuba's external debt, it is crucial to examine the history and causes of the country's debt crisis, as well as the strategies employed by the Cuban government to manage these challenges.

Cuba's external debt has had a profound impact on the country's economic development. The accumulation of debt has limited the government's ability to invest in public services and social welfare programs, hindering the overall well-being of the population. Understanding the implications of this debt on social welfare and public services is essential for bankers to assess the country's financial stability.

International financial institutions have played a crucial role in Cuba's debt refinancing efforts. Analyzing their involvement and assessing their impact on the country's debt management strategies is vital for bankers looking to evaluate the potential risks and benefits of engaging with Cuba.

Moreover, Cuba's external debt has also affected the inflow of foreign direct investment (FDI). By exploring the relationship between external debt and FDI, bankers can gain insights into the challenges and opportunities for investment in the country.

Additionally, Cuba's external debt has implications for domestic inflation and currency stability. Understanding the impact of debt on these factors is essential for bankers to assess the risks associated with lending and investing in the country.

The subchapter also examines the implications of Cuba's external debt on the country's credit rating. A thorough analysis of the factors influencing the credit rating can provide bankers with insights into the country's creditworthiness and potential risks involved in lending to Cuba.

Furthermore, the subchapter delves into the analysis of Cuba's debt restructuring and negotiation processes with creditors. Understanding the patterns and outcomes of these negotiations can provide invaluable insights into potential solutions for long-term debt sustainability.

In conclusion, forecasting Cuba's external debt sustainability requires a comprehensive analysis of multiple factors, including the country's debt crisis history, government strategies, social welfare implications, international financial institution involvement, FDI impact, inflation and currency stability, credit rating implications, and debt restructuring processes. By examining these aspects, bankers can gain a deeper understanding of the challenges and opportunities associated with Cuba's external debt and develop potential solutions for long-term sustainability.

Potential Solutions for Long-term Debt Sustainability

In order to address the long-term debt sustainability challenges faced by Cuba, several potential solutions can be considered. These solutions aim to alleviate the burden of external debt and create a more sustainable financial environment for the country.

1. Debt Restructuring and Negotiation: Cuba can engage in negotiations with its creditors to restructure its debt. This process involves extending the maturity dates, reducing interest rates, and possibly forgiving a portion of the debt. By renegotiating the terms of the debt, Cuba can alleviate its immediate financial pressures and create a more manageable repayment plan.

2. Economic Diversification: Cuba can focus on diversifying its economy to reduce its dependence on a few key industries. By promoting sectors such as tourism, manufacturing, and technology, the country can generate additional revenue streams and reduce its reliance on external borrowing. This approach can help improve the country's ability to generate income and repay its debt in the long run.

3. Foreign Direct Investment: Encouraging foreign direct investment can provide Cuba with the necessary capital to address its debt sustainability challenges. By attracting investors, the country can access new sources of financing, stimulate economic growth, and create employment opportunities. This influx of foreign investment can also help Cuba generate the necessary funds to repay its external debt.

4. Strengthening Public Finances: Cuba can implement measures to improve its fiscal discipline and strengthen its public finances. This can include reducing government spending, increasing tax revenues, and implementing effective budgetary controls. By managing its finances more prudently, the country can create a surplus, which can be used to repay its debt obligations.

5. Collaboration with International Fibancial Institutions: Cuba can seek assistance from international financial institutions, such as the International Monetary Fund (IMF) or the World Bank, to develop strategies for debt management and access to financial resources. These institutions can provide technical expertise, financial resources, and policy advice to help Cuba navigate its debt sustainability challenges.

Overall, addressing the long-term debt sustainability challenges faced by Cuba requires a comprehensive and multi-faceted approach. By implementing debt restructuring, diversifying the economy, attracting foreign direct investment, strengthening public finances, and collaborating with international financial institutions, Cuba can work towards achieving long-term debt sustainability and promoting economic development for the benefit of its people.

Recommendations for Policy-makers and Stakeholders

As Cuba continues to grapple with its external debt crisis, it is imperative for policy-makers and stakeholders to actively engage in finding solutions that promote long-term sustainability and economic development. This subchapter aims to provide recommendations for policy-makers and stakeholders in addressing the various challenges posed by Cuba's external debt crisis.

Firstly, policy-makers should prioritize the implementation of comprehensive debt management strategies. This includes establishing clear guidelines for debt issuance, monitoring and evaluating debt levels, and developing risk management mechanisms to mitigate future debt crises. Policy-makers should also explore avenues for debt restructuring and negotiate with creditors in a transparent and efficient manner.

Furthermore, policy-makers should actively seek external assistance from international financial institutions (IFIs) to support Cuba in its debt refinancing efforts. IFIs can provide technical expertise, financial resources, and policy advice to help Cuba navigate the complexities of debt management and find sustainable solutions. Collaborating with IFIs can also enhance Cuba's credibility and improve its access to international capital markets.

Stakeholders, particularly bankers, should play a proactive role in supporting Cuba's efforts to manage its external debt and delinquencies.

This can be done by offering financial expertise and resources to assist in debt restructuring negotiations, providing technical assistance in implementing effective debt management strategies, and facilitating access to international capital markets.

Moreover, stakeholders should encourage and support foreign direct investment (FDI) in Cuba. FDI can help alleviate the burden of external debt by injecting much-needed capital into the economy, fostering job creation, and promoting economic growth. Stakeholders can provide guidance to potential investors, highlighting the investment opportunities and potential returns in Cuba.

It is also crucial for policy-makers and stakeholders to address the social implications of Cuba's external debt crisis. They should prioritize the allocation of resources towards social welfare programs and public services to ensure that the most vulnerable segments of society are not disproportionately affected. Additionally, policy-makers should implement measures to mitigate the impact of external debt on domestic inflation and currency stability, to safeguard the purchasing power of the population.

In conclusion, by implementing these recommendations, policy-makers and stakeholders can contribute to the long-term sustainability and economic development of Cuba. Collaboration, transparency, and a proactive approach are key to finding effective solutions to Cuba's external debt crisis and ensuring a prosperous future for the country.

Chapter 14: Conclusion

Recap of Key Findings and Insights

In this subchapter, we will provide a recap of the key findings and insights presented throughout the book, "Unraveling the History and Causes of Cuba's External Debt Crisis: A Banker's Perspective." This recap aims to provide a concise overview for bankers who are interested in understanding the nuances of Cuba's external debt crisis and its implications on various aspects of the country's economy.

One of the primary findings discussed in this book is the magnitude of Cuba's external debt and the challenges it poses for the country's economic development. The historical analysis revealed that Cuba's external debt has been a persistent issue, and the accumulation of delinquencies and refinancing difficulties has hindered the country's progress. These challenges have also impacted the social welfare of the Cuban population, as the government has had to divert resources from public services to meet its debt obligations.

The book also sheds light on the Cuban government's strategies for managing external debt and delinquencies. It explores the various approaches employed by the government, including debt restructuring and negotiation processes with creditors. Additionally, the role of international financial institutions in assisting Cuba with its debt refinancing efforts is examined, highlighting their significance in providing support and guidance.

Moreover, the impact of Cuba's external debt on foreign direct investment and domestic inflation is thoroughly analyzed. The book reveals that the high level of debt discourages foreign investors, as it raises concerns about the country's ability to meet financial obligations.

Furthermore, the debt burden contributes to domestic inflation and poses challenges to currency stability.

The implications of Cuba's external debt on the country's credit rating are also explored in this book. It discusses how the debt crisis has resulted in downgrades in credit ratings, limiting Cuba's access to international capital markets and exacerbating its financial challenges.

Lastly, the book offers insights into the future prospects for Cuba's external debt and potential solutions for long-term sustainability. It emphasizes the importance of implementing comprehensive reforms, such as enhancing transparency and accountability, diversifying the economy, and attracting foreign investment, to address the root causes of the debt crisis.

Overall, this subchapter serves as a summary of the key findings and insights presented in the book, providing bankers with a comprehensive understanding of Cuba's external debt crisis and potential strategies for long-term sustainability.

Implications for Bankers and Financial Institutions

The implications of Cuba's external debt crisis for bankers and financial institutions cannot be understated. As key stakeholders in the global financial system, bankers must carefully assess the risks and opportunities associated with Cuba's external debt, delinquencies, and refinancing difficulties.

One of the primary concerns for bankers is the impact of Cuba's external debt on economic development. As the country struggles to meet its debt obligations, it may face limitations in funding essential infrastructure projects and investment opportunities. This, in turn, could hamper economic growth and limit potential business prospects for financial institutions operating in Cuba.

Moreover, the history and causes of Cuba's external debt crisis must be thoroughly understood by bankers in order to make informed decisions. By examining the root causes of the crisis, bankers can better assess the likelihood of future delinquencies and the potential for debt restructuring or negotiation processes. This knowledge is crucial for managing risk and minimizing potential losses.

The Cuban government's strategies for managing external debt and delinquencies also have far-reaching implications for bankers. Any changes in debt repayment plans, refinancing efforts, or debt restructuring can directly impact the financial institutions involved. It is therefore essential for bankers to closely monitor and analyze these strategies to accurately assess their potential implications.

The role of international financial institutions in Cuba's debt refinancing efforts is another important consideration for bankers. Collaborations between Cuba and international financial institutions can provide opportunities for financial institutions to participate in debt restructuring processes and potentially mitigate risks associated with Cuba's external debt.

Furthermore, bankers must evaluate how Cuba's external debt may affect foreign direct investment (FDI) in the country. High levels of external debt can deter potential investors, as it raises concerns about the country's ability to meet its financial obligations. This, in turn, can impact the availability of investment opportunities for financial institutions and their clients.

Additionally, bankers need to be aware of the potential impact of Cuba's external debt on domestic inflation and currency stability. If the country struggles to manage its debt, it may resort to inflationary measures or currency devaluation, both of which can have significant consequences for financial institutions operating in Cuba.

The implications of Cuba's external debt on the country's credit rating must also be considered. A downgrade in Cuba's credit rating can increase borrowing costs and limit access to international financial markets. Bankers must closely monitor any changes in Cuba's credit rating and adjust their strategies accordingly.

Finally, bankers should explore potential long-term solutions for Cuba's external debt sustainability. This includes analyzing debt restructuring and negotiation processes with creditors, as well as identifying future prospects for debt management. Developing innovative financial instruments and exploring alternative sources of funding can also contribute to long-term sustainability.

In conclusion, bankers and financial institutions must carefully consider the implications of Cuba's external debt crisis. By understanding the impact on economic development, social welfare, credit ratings, and foreign direct investment, bankers can navigate the challenges and opportunities presented by Cuba's external debt, while also contributing to long-term solutions for debt sustainability.

Final Thoughts on Cuba's External Debt Crisis

The external debt crisis in Cuba has had far-reaching implications for the country's economic development and social welfare. This chapter has provided a comprehensive analysis of the history and causes of Cuba's external debt crisis, as well as the strategies employed by the Cuban government to manage debt and delinquencies.

One of the key takeaways from this exploration is the significant impact that Cuba's external debt has had on its economic development. The country has faced numerous challenges in financing its debt obligations, resulting in a lack of funds for public services and social welfare programs. This has had a direct impact on the quality of life for the

Cuban people, with limited access to basic necessities and reduced government spending on education and healthcare.

In addition, the role of international financial institutions in Cuba's debt refinancing efforts cannot be overlooked. Despite the challenges, these institutions have played a crucial role in providing financial support and negotiating debt restructuring agreements. Their involvement has helped to alleviate some of the burden on the Cuban government and create opportunities for long-term sustainability.

However, it is important to recognize that Cuba's external debt crisis has also had negative implications for foreign direct investment. The uncertainty surrounding the country's debt situation has made investors hesitant to commit capital, resulting in a slowdown in economic growth and development.

Furthermore, the impact of Cuba's external debt on domestic inflation and currency stability cannot be ignored. The country has faced challenges in maintaining price stability and managing its currency, which has led to increased inflation and currency depreciation. These factors have further exacerbated the economic challenges facing the Cuban government.

Looking ahead, it is clear that Cuba's external debt crisis requires long-term solutions for sustainability. The country must continue to prioritize debt restructuring and negotiation processes with creditors, while also exploring alternative sources of financing and investment. This will require a concerted effort from both the Cuban government and international financial institutions to ensure a stable and prosperous future for the country.

In conclusion, the external debt crisis in Cuba has had a profound impact on the country's economic development, social welfare, and credit rating. The challenges faced by the Cuban government in managing debt and delinquencies have necessitated the involvement of international financial institutions and a strategic approach to debt restructuring. Moving forward, it is crucial for Cuba to explore sustainable solutions and prioritize long-term economic stability in order to overcome its external debt crisis and pave the way for a prosperous future.

www.ingramcontent.com/pod-product-compliance
Lightning Source LLC
Chambersburg PA
CBHW051244160726
47994CB00003B/1022